The Victorious Walk

A Handbook for the Believer's Victory

Gary V. Whetstone

Gary Whetstone Publishing
New Castle, Delaware

What Christian Leaders Are Saying about the Ministry of Gary V. Whetstone

"…I have been in the pulpits of the world with Gary Whetstone, and…my personal witness of the anointing and the power that God uses through him literally changes lives. …The quality and the depth of his teaching, its interdenominational flavor, its anointed power is something that I…encourage you to take advantage of."

Charles Blair
Calvary Temple in Denver, CO

"…The level of teaching that [Pastor Gary Whetstone] brings to the table is absolutely incredible! You need this. It's going to take you to the next level…. When you get an opportunity to hear something that Pastor Whetstone has endorsed and prepared, you are dealing with somebody who's not just been in the boardroom, but has been right there on the field fighting…and he knows what he's talking about."

T.D. Jakes
The Potter's House

"Gary and Faye Whetstone attended our church in Tulsa before they began the powerful work that they now have in Delaware. We're excited for the new Bible training they have, to put God's Word practically into people's lives. They have a vision to reach the world for Jesus Christ…. We recommend highly what Gary and Faye Whetstone are doing in this new Bible Study training. Get plugged in!"

Billy Joe Daugherty
Victory Christian Center in Tulsa, OK

"...It's indeed a great honor...to talk to you about the incredible biblical study program under the anointed leadership of Gary Whetstone. First, I have known Gary for many, many years. Gary is an incredible pastor and teacher and evangelist to the nations of the world, and is spiritually qualified to head up this marvelous biblical study.... I wholeheartedly recommend this biblical study ministry under the leadership of Gary Whetstone...."

Morris Cerullo
World Evangelism, Inc.

"...I believe all those who sit under this anointed teaching...and the ministry of Pastor Whetstone at this remarkable school will be thoroughly equipped to gather in the end-time harvest before the imminent return of our Lord and Savior Jesus Christ."

Rod Parsley
World Harvest Church

Gary Whetstone Publishing
P.O. Box 10050
Wilmington, DE 19850 U.S.A.
PHONE: (302) 561-6800
TOLL-FREE: (800) 383-4223
FAX: (302) 324-5448
WEB SITE: www.JesusExperience.com
E-MAIL: info@JesusExperience.com

Some scriptures have been italicized for emphasis.

ISBN 0-9664462-0-8 English
ISBN 0-9664462-9-1 Spanish (Español)
ISBN 1-58866-252-7 English eBook

Contents

Introduction

This handbook is vital to you as a believer. In your journey through *The Victorious Walk,* you will find that the revelation of God's Word is the foundation of all truth in your life. These truths will bring you personal freedom and a great desire to study and understand His Word. The Bible says:

> Be diligent to present yourself approved to God, a worker who does not need to be ashamed, rightly dividing the word of truth.
>
> 2 Timothy 2:15

What you are about to read and act upon will chart the course of your whole life! Jesus said:

> I have come that they may have life, and that they may have it more abundantly.
>
> John 10:10b

Every believer has the right to:

- Abundant life
- Health, mental stability, and well-being
- The supernatural abundance of God in finances
- Peace in relationships
- And all the promises of God contained in the Bible.

These are your God-given rights. However, Satan attempts to destroy God's plan. By influence of the devil, man has created godless religious doctrines and has brought confusion to the simplicity of the Bible. In this way, Satan successfully has withheld from the Body of Christ—the Church—many of the benefits that are ours through our Lord Jesus Christ.

> Bless the LORD, O my soul,
> And forget not all His benefits.
>
> Psalm 103:2

You must realize, activate, and experience God's benefits in your life. To do this, first understand that His promises always are available to you. Then, you need to begin reading and studying the Bible to know what these benefits are. As you go through this book, you will learn principles to help you activate the Word of God in your life. Reading the Scriptures and praying aloud the prayers at the end of the chapters will help you to walk with the Lord. When prayer and study become part of your daily routine, you will have a Victorious Walk with Jesus every day!

As you embark on the journey of The Victorious Walk, I pray today that you will discover and experience every benefit of God in this book. His Word is alive! God calls you through biblical principles to experience The Victorious Walk!

1
What Is the New Birth?

As you journey with me in understanding the *new birth*, realize that the enemy has tried to keep you from this discovery. Man's religion has clouded and obscured the revelation of the new life of Christ, which God desires to give to you freely by grace.

You Are a New Creation

When an infant is born physically into the world, he begins to discover all the faculties and strengths he will enjoy in life. Especially in the first three formative years of life, a baby develops in his communication and relationship with the environment. Similarly, a believer who is newly born again spiritually begins an incredible learning process. He starts to understand the *revelation*—which means the act of discovering or taking off the cover—of who Jesus is and how to walk as a child of God.

You see, being born again is a spiritual rebirth. Jesus explained it this way:

> "...Unless one is born of water [God's Word] and the Spirit, he cannot enter the kingdom of God.
> "That which is born of the flesh is flesh, and that which is born of the Spirit is spirit."
>
> John 3:5-6

Jesus provided a way for you to become God's child by exchanging His life for yours:

3

> But as many as received Him [Jesus], to them *He gave the right to become children of God,* even to those who believe in His name:
> who were born, not of blood, nor of the will of the flesh, *nor of the will of man, but of God.*
>
> John 1:12-13

Understand that although you must choose to receive the Lord Jesus Christ, it is not your will but God's will that causes you to become born again.

When you accept Christ, realize that you become *a new creation.* This is new birth. In the Bible, the Apostle Paul taught:

> Therefore, *if anyone is in Christ, he is a new creation;* old things have passed away; behold, all things have become new.
> Now all things are of God, who has reconciled us to Himself through Jesus Christ....
>
> 2 Corinthians 5:17-18

When you are born again, you become a brand-new person. You are alive in Jesus Christ, created after His image.

> And have put on *the new man* who is renewed in knowledge *according to the image of Him who created him.*
>
> Colossians 3:10

Your heart becomes like Jesus. You become grafted into Christ Himself. As a believer, you become united with Him as a branch connects to a vine. Jesus taught:

4

"I am the vine, you are the branches. He who abides in Me, and I in him, bears much fruit; for without Me you can do nothing."

John 15:5

You Are Righteous in Christ

Righteousness is another benefit of the new birth. This gift is the ability to stand in the presence of God without any sense of guilt or inferiority, as if sin had never existed in your life. You may be thinking, *How can anyone call me "righteous"? You don't know what I have done.*

The Bible tells us that when you believe and accept Jesus into your life, you become righteous, or receive right standing with God, your Father:

> ...He [God] made Him [Jesus] who knew no sin to be sin for us, that we might become the righteousness of God in Him.

2 Corinthians 5:21

You may feel tempted to become right with God by doing religious works. Yet, no matter how hard you try, it is impossible to earn salvation through your own efforts. This is Jesus' accomplishment. Salvation is not of man, but of God. Salvation is Jesus' finished work. He showered you with grace and purchased you by His blood. He paid the price for you with His shed blood on the cross. The Bible explains it this way:

> You were bought at a price; do not become slaves of men.

1 Corinthians 7:23

On the cross of Calvary, Jesus was *the Son of Man made* sin *on your behalf.* Jesus, *in resurrection,* is *the Son of Man made* righteous *on your behalf.*

When Jesus purchased you by going to the cross of Calvary, He exchanged His sinless life for yours. It is as if He put His spotless robe of purity upon you, and took for Himself your tattered coat of sin. He gave to you the gift of His righteousness—His right standing with God. Through the cross, Jesus took upon Himself **all** your accusations, guilt, shame, and self-condemnation.

Jesus Is Your New Lord

Jesus is perfectly capable of protecting and keeping that which He has purchased:

> For He Himself has said, "I will never leave you nor forsake you."
>
> Hebrews 13:5b

Stand in the celebration of His finished work! Realize that when you accept Christ, the devil—your spiritual enemy—no longer has authority over you. You leave his kingdom and move into God's Kingdom!

> He has delivered us from the power of darkness and translated us into the kingdom of the Son of His love.
>
> Colossians 1:13

In effect, you have changed landlords! Jesus is now the Lord over your life, and He said:

> ..."All authority has been given to Me in heaven and on earth."
>
> Matthew 28:18

Understand that Satan no longer has authority over you (unless you allow it).

> For you did not receive the spirit of bondage again to fear, but you received the Spirit of adoption by whom we cry out, "Abba, Father."
>
> Romans 8:15

Jesus paid the price and now owns you.

> Or do you not know that your body is the temple of the Holy Spirit who is in you, whom you have from God, and you are not your own?
>
> 1 Corinthians 6:19

Jesus explained that His blood has washed away **all** your sins:

> "For this is My blood of the new covenant, which is shed for many for the remission of sins."
>
> Matthew 26:28

> And you know that He was manifested to take away our sins, and in Him there is no sin.
>
> 1 John 3:5

Repentance Changes Your Direction

When you accept Jesus and acknowledge Him as your personal Savior, you are just beginning your life with Him. This is where true biblical repentance works in your heart and mind. *Repentance* simply means choosing to turn around to go the correct direction. When you turn away from sin and the ways of sinful flesh to obey

God's Word, you have repented. You have turned from living in the devil's kingdom to God's Kingdom.

Renew Your Mind

The next step is the renewing of your mind with God's Word. This causes you to become mature in the Lord.

> I beseech you therefore, brethren, by the mercies of God, that you present your bodies a living sacrifice, holy, acceptable to God, which is your reasonable service.
>
> And do not be conformed to this world, but be transformed by the renewing of your mind, that you may prove what is that good and acceptable and perfect will of God.
>
> Romans 12:1-2

The Bible says that if you are a Christian, you should not act like the world in its sinful ways. We know that it is possible, as a believer, to act in worldly ways.

How do you renew your mind and gain spiritual strength and maturity?

1. Let the Word of God cleanse your mind.

> That He might sanctify and cleanse it with the washing of water by the word.
>
> Ephesians 5:26

Use a Bible in a translation that is easy to understand, in which you can highlight or underline passages that are especially meaningful. Read your Bible daily and meditate on the Scriptures, rehearsing them over and over until they take root in your heart. If you are a new Christian, begin by reading the book of Luke.

Soon, revelation will dawn on your heart, and wisdom from the truth of God's Word will penetrate your spirit. The anointing—the power and presence of the Holy Spirit of God—will become your personal Teacher:

> But the anointing which you have received from Him abides in you, and you do not need that anyone teach you; but as the same anointing teaches you concerning all things, and is true, and is not a lie, and just as it has taught you, you will abide in Him.
>
> 1 John 2:27

As you daily read His Word and spend time meditating on it, God will reveal truths to you about your new life in Christ. The biblical revelation of *meditation* means to mutter the Scriptures by speaking them over and over aloud to yourself. When you do this, you begin to understand more fully the depths of God's truths.

Consider a physical example to illustrate the spiritual principle of meditation. Let's say a rough stone begins a journey in a mountain stream, flows into a river, and ultimately reaches the ocean. As the rock tumbles over and over thousands of times on this trip, eventually all its rough edges wear off, revealing a smooth core. By examination, then, one can see into the stone's core without obstructions. Similarly, when you meditate on the Bible, the Spirit of God pierces through the rough edges of your own thoughts, attitudes, and behaviors. This allows you to see more clearly the core truths of God.

2. Find a Bible-believing church, which teaches the uncompromising Word of God.

> Not forsaking the assembling of ourselves together....
>
> Hebrews 10:25

Attend the services regularly and become involved in some area or activity of the church. Since the Holy Spirit sets believers in the church, He will lead you to the church God wants you to attend.

> But now God has set the members, each one of them, in the body just as He pleased.
>
> 1 Corinthians 12:18

3. Know that God will complete the good work, which He started in you.

> Being confident of this very thing, that He who has begun a good work in you will complete it until the day of Jesus Christ.
>
> Philippians 1:6

You Are Victorious

Isn't it exciting to know that God did for you what you could not do for yourself? When you accept Christ He makes you a winner, an overcomer, more than a conqueror, the head and not the tail, and above and not beneath. Moses declared:

> "And the LORD will make you the head and not the tail; you shall be above only, and not be beneath, if you heed the commandments of the LORD your God, which I command you today, and are careful to observe them."
>
> Deuteronomy 28:13

God makes you triumphant and prosperous in everything you endeavor.

Now thanks be to God who always leads us in triumph in Christ, and through us diffuses the fragrance of His knowledge in every place.

2 Corinthians 2:14

Be Confident of Eternal Life

God's Word promises assurance of your salvation!

And this is the testimony: that God has given us eternal life, and this life is in His Son.

He who has the Son has life; he who does not have the Son of God does not have life.

These things I have written to you who believe in the name of the Son of God, that you may know that you have eternal life, and that you may continue to believe in the name of the Son of God.

1 John 5:11-13

This is exciting news! If you have God's Son, the Lord Jesus Christ, you have life. We do not establish our salvation on feelings, emotions, or even on church membership. **Our foundation is the Word of God.** When you accept Christ, God's Spirit confirms within your spirit that you are His child:

The Spirit Himself bears witness with our spirit that we are the children of God.

Romans 8:16

When we meet His conditions—repent, believe in Jesus and confess Him as Lord—we have confidence that we are saved.

> For you were bought at a price; therefore glorify God
> in your body and in your spirit, which are God's.
>
> 1 Corinthians 6:20

Isn't it comforting to know that Jesus took our places at Calvary, so we could have eternal life!

Be Born Again

If you have not accepted Jesus Christ as your Lord and Savior, you can do this, right now. The Bible explains how you can be born again:

> …If you *confess with your mouth* the Lord Jesus *and believe in your heart* that God has raised Him from the dead, you will be saved.
> For with the heart one believes to righteousness, and with the mouth confession is made to salvation.
>
> Romans 10:9-10

If you have not prayed a simple prayer to confess Jesus, do it now and God promises that you will receive eternal life. Say this aloud:

> **Father, thank You for loving me. Thank You for sending Your Son, Jesus, to die and rise from the dead for me. Right now, I repent of all my sins. By Jesus' Blood, I ask You to forgive me. I receive Him into my heart and confess that Jesus is Lord and Savior of my life. In Jesus' Name. Amen.**

Just now, if you sincerely prayed this, you became born again into God's family and Kingdom! The moment you confessed that

Jesus is your Lord and Savior, God took you out of the kingdom of darkness where Satan rules. He placed you into His Kingdom where He rules and reigns forever. Congratulations! You have become a child of God.

Scriptural Confessions of Faith

The following prayers will help you to strengthen your faith as you pray the Word of God. In each section below, read the Scripture first, then activate God's Word by speaking aloud the following prayer in bold letters.

The Spirit Himself bears witness with our spirit that we are children of God,
and if children, then heirs—heirs of God and joint heirs with Christ....

Romans 8:16-17

Father, I thank You that Your Holy Spirit bears witness with my spirit that I am born of You. I have Your life and nature, my God, inside me. I am Your child. Therefore, I am Your heir, Father, and a joint heir with Christ.

There is therefore now no condemnation to those who are in Christ Jesus, who do not walk according to the flesh, but according to the Spirit.

Romans 8:1

Christ Jesus, I am in You. In Your power, I walk according to the Spirit of God and not according to my flesh. Therefore, I am free from condemnation.

For we are His workmanship, created in Christ Jesus for good works, which God prepared beforehand that we should walk in them.

Ephesians 2:10

Father, thank You that I am a new creation. You recreated me in the Person of Jesus Christ. I realize that I am Your workmanship. Thank You for anointing and appointing me to do successful "good works" by Your power for Your glory.

For as many as are led by the Spirit of God, these are sons of God.

Romans 8:14

Father, I am Your child—a child of Light. I expect Your Holy Spirit to guide me. I believe, in Jesus' Name, that You are leading me now.

Jesus said:

"Therefore if the Son makes you free, you shall be free indeed."

John 8:36

I am free from all guilt, shame, insecurity, inferiority, accusation, and torment from my past. Thank You, Jesus, for setting me free! In Jesus' Name. Amen.

2
What Is Faith?

You may feel that you haven't had the faith to succeed in your everyday routine or to face life's greatest challenges. However, what you have missed in the past due possibly to a lack of understanding will be revealed in this chapter! As you continue in this book, open your heart to discover the biblical understanding of faith. Faith is God's key to The Victorious Walk.

You must realize that if you are a child of God, you already have all the faith necessary to overcome every obstacle! You currently possess the knowledge to walk with God and experience His intervention in your life. This revelation about faith is the anchor that will help you to understand and experience God's promises. As a Christian, faith is your divine connection to the throne of God.

How do you know faith will work? It is because God promised it, and He does not lie.

What Is Faith?

First, you need to discover what faith is and why you need it. Faith is having the assurance that what you hope for will happen because of God's eternal, unchanging Word. Faith is also having an absolute belief that what God says in the Bible is true.

> Now faith is the substance of things hoped for, the evidence of things not seen.
>
> Hebrews 11:1

Now, what you ask and hope for must be according to God's Word. God is honorable, and He honors His promises. However, if you pray for something contrary to the Bible, God cannot honor it, because He did not promise it.

Where Does Faith Come From?

God has given to you a measure of faith. It is His gift to you. In fact, He has given to every Christian the same measure of faith. Each of us has the potential and ability to exercise and develop that faith.

> For I say, through the grace given to me, to everyone who is among you, not to think of himself more highly than he ought to think, but to think soberly, as God has dealt to each one *a measure of faith.*
>
> Romans 12:3

How Do You Strengthen Your Faith?

You strengthen and grow your measure of faith by God's Word. The more you read, hear, and understand the Bible, the greater your faith grows.

> So then faith comes by hearing, and hearing by the word of God.
>
> Romans 10:17

How Do You Activate Your Faith?

Your faith requires corresponding action. This is essential. God will honor your faith when you *believe and act* upon it.

For as the body without the spirit is dead, *so faith without works [or corresponding actions] is dead also.*

James 2:26

Your corresponding works or actions activate your faith.

Speak Your Faith

What you believe and say demonstrates your faith.

But since we have the same spirit of faith, according to what is written, *"I believed and therefore I spoke,"* we also believe and therefore speak.

2 Corinthians 4:13

You see, faith operates upon the foundation of God's Word. The Bible declares that when you believe and speak God's promises, they manifest in your life. Speaking according to your faith is an action that activates your faith. Jesus said:

"For assuredly, I say to you, whoever says to this mountain, 'Be removed, and be cast into the sea' and does not doubt in his heart, but *believes that those things he says will come to pass, he will have whatever he says.*

"Therefore I say to you, whatever things you ask *when you pray, believe that you receive them, and you will have them."*

Mark 11:23-24

In Chapter 10 of Mark, a blind man named Bartimaeus received his healing, because he came to Jesus, believing and asking for his sight:

And Jesus answered and said to him, "What do you want Me to do for you?" The blind man said to Him, "Rabboni [which means Master], that I may receive my sight."

Then Jesus said to him, "Go your way; *your faith has made you well.*" And immediately he received his sight and followed Jesus on the road.

Mark 10:51-52

Bartimaeus' corresponding actions and speech activated his faith for his miracle.

Through Faith—Not Works—You Obtain God's Promises

All God's promises are available to you through faith. In fact, you received salvation, because you *confessed your faith* in God and the finished work of Jesus. Although you had corresponding works—your confession of faith—it was *through your faith* not *the works* that you were saved.

For by grace you have been saved through *faith,* and that not of yourselves; it is the gift of God, *not of works,* lest anyone should boast.

Ephesians 2:8-9

It is His will for all to use their faith to be saved. When you received salvation by believing and then speaking the Word of God, you activated the faith principle. Here, let me quote a passage of Scripture, part of which we studied in the previous chapter. This clarifies how to activate your faith regarding salvation:

But what does it say? "The word is near you, even in

18

your mouth and in your heart" (that is, *the word of faith* which we preach):

that if you *confess with your mouth* the Lord Jesus and *believe in your heart* that God has raised Him from the dead, you will be saved.

For with the heart one believes to righteousness, and with the mouth confession is made to salvation.

Romans 10:8-10

Due to false religious beliefs, many have not understood that righteousness—right standing with God—comes through *faith* when they believe and confess Jesus as Lord. Remember, the definition of *righteousness* is the ability to stand in the presence of God without the sense of guilt or inferiority—as though sin had never existed! Many believe the devil's lie that they must work to be righteous. No, they must only believe. This is one of the enemy's easiest ways to steal people's joy: They fall into the very burdensome trap of working to be right with God.

Even the righteousness of God...is through faith in Jesus Christ to all and on all who believe....

Romans 3:22

God hears and answers the prayers of His righteous children. First, He *makes* you righteous. Then, because you are righteous, He answers your prayers! This is only one of the many benefits you receive through faith in Jesus Christ.

The effective, fervent prayer of a *righteous* man avails much.

James 5:16b

What Can You Expect from Your Faith?

You can count on results when you act according to your faith.

1. Expect immediate results.

We enjoy quick answers to our prayers of faith, and sometimes we get them. However, we *always* get our answers in God's perfect timing. In the meantime, we receive other results. (See list below.)

2. Expect patience.

Patience enables you to commit long-term to believing for answered prayers. This develops an important "fruit of the Spirit," which is the result of the Holy Spirit's work in your life:

> But the fruit of the Spirit is love, joy, peace, *patience,* kindness, goodness, faithfulness, gentleness and self-control. Against such things there is no law.
>
> Galatians 5:22-23 (NIV)

One of your goals as a Christian should be to become more Christ-like by growing in the fruit of the Spirit.

3. Expect tribulation.

When you step into faith, it is common to experience tribulation (pressures and resistance). Do not be discouraged when you face difficulties with your faith walk. Every believer does. That is why the Bible calls it the "fight of faith":

> *Fight the good fight of faith,* lay hold on eternal life, to which you were also called and have confessed the good confession in the presence of many witnesses.
>
> 1 Timothy 6:12

It is common for every one of us to "fight the good fight of faith." While obstacles and opponents resist you, God's Word guarantees that through faith and patience you will inherit His promises:

> That you do not become sluggish, but imitate those who *through faith and patience inherit the promises.*
>
> Hebrews 6:12

Now, do you see why you need patience? As a seed planted in the ground takes time to grow, so also faith planted in the heart takes time to produce its results. Be patient. You will overcome every obstacle, because your faith is the victory that overcomes the world!

> For whatever is born of God overcomes the world. And this is the victory that has overcome the world—our faith.
>
> 1 John 5:4

Scriptural Confessions of Faith

Remember, you activate your faith by believing and speaking God's Word. This causes the Word to come alive in your heart. Read the following Scriptures and confess them aloud (in bold letters) to activate your faith. This will help your faith to grow stronger. Then, find other Scriptures that promise answers to challenges in your and others' lives. Activate your faith by speaking them into existence. This is how to walk in victory.

> For in Christ Jesus neither circumcision nor uncircumcision avails anything, but a *new creation.*
>
> Galatians 6:15

Father, when I became born again, my spirit was reborn. I am a new creation, because my spirit received the same life that abides in You and in Christ Jesus. I prevail!

Therefore, if anyone is in Christ, he is a new creation; old things have passed away; behold, all things have become new.

Now all things are of God, who has reconciled us to Himself through Jesus Christ, and has given us the ministry of reconciliation [coming back into fellowship or harmony with God],

that is, that God was in Christ reconciling the world to Himself, not imputing their trespasses to them, and has committed to us the word of reconciliation.

Therefore we are ambassadors for Christ, as though God were pleading through us: we implore you on Christ's behalf, be reconciled to God.

For He made Him who knew no sin to be sin for us, that we might become the righteousness of God in Him.

2 Corinthians 5:17-21

I am in Christ and in union with Him. I am a new creation. Old things have passed away and all things have become new. Father, now I am Your righteousness in Christ. Thank You, God, for reconciling me to Yourself and for giving to me the ministry of reconciliation. Through my words and deeds, I am causing others to come into peace and harmony with You. I am an ambassador for Christ. I minister healing to others.

"I have been crucified with Christ; it is no longer I who

live, but Christ lives in me; and the life which I now live in the flesh I live by faith in the Son of God, who loved me and gave Himself for me."

Galatians 2:20

For you died, and your life is hidden with Christ in God.

Colossians 3:3

Jesus, through Your death, I have died to the flesh. Therefore, I have died to sin and the desires and values of the world. My life is now hidden with You in God. Now, You live Your life through me!

Let the word of Christ dwell in you richly in all wisdom, teaching and admonishing one another in psalms and hymns and spiritual songs, singing with grace in your hearts to the Lord.

Colossians 3:16

The Word of Christ now dwells in my heart and mind. His Word springs up in me in all fullness. It teaches, admonishes, and trains me. This Word teaches wisdom to me in spiritual and natural matters. I sing psalms, hymns, and spiritual songs, which glorify and praise my Father, God.

[God]…raised us up together, and made us sit together in heavenly places in Christ Jesus.

Ephesians 2:6

Which He [God] worked in Christ when He raised

Him from the dead and seated Him at His right hand in the heavenly places,

far above all principality and power and might and dominion, and every name that is named, not only in this age but also in that which is to come.

Ephesians 1:20-21

Father, thank You for raising me up with Christ Jesus when You raised Him from the dead. Thank You for making it possible for me to sit with Him in heavenly places—even now. In Jesus, I sit at Your right hand, far above all principality and power and might and dominion, and every name that is named, now and forevermore.

God, my Father, I fully expect You to do exactly what Your Word in the Bible says You will do. I also praise and worship You, because I am in You and You are in me. In Jesus' Name. Amen.

3
The Holy Spirit and You

Can you imagine selling electrical appliances to a country that has no electricity? No one would buy them, because the power to operate the appliances would not be available. So it is with many Christians. They have God's promises in a powerless life.

However, God did not give His promises to you without the power to make them work. You see, He sent the Holy Spirit, the power of God, to activate His blessings in your life. God gave the Holy Spirit to you as a gift at salvation. However, He also promised that the Holy Spirit would *overflow* through you in power!

As we take the next steps through *The Victorious Walk*, you can experience the indwelling presence of the Holy Spirit and the release of His awesome power.

Who Is this Baptism For?

Every believer receives the Holy Spirit at his new birth. From our studies in the previous chapters, we learned that the new birth means a believer is born again of the Spirit of God. However, this is not the Baptism in the Holy Spirit.

After salvation, God promises power to new believers. This promise of the Father is the Baptism in the Holy Spirit. Immediately before His ascension into Heaven, Jesus told His disciples:

> "Behold, I send the *Promise of My Father* upon you; but tarry in the city of Jerusalem until you are *endued with power from on high.*"
>
> Luke 24:49

Another verse confirms this:

And being assembled together with them [the apostles],
He [Jesus] commanded them not to depart from Jerusalem,
but to *wait for the Promise of the Father*, "which," He said,
"you have heard from Me."

Acts 1:4

Although the born-again believer has received the Holy Spirit
at the new birth, the Baptism in the Holy Spirit is a separate
experience. Any Christian can receive this baptism. God first poured
out His Holy Spirit on the day of Pentecost (Acts 2), and the Spirit
has never left. In explaining the first occurrences of the Baptism
in the Holy Spirit on Pentecost, Peter declared:

"[Jesus] Therefore being exalted to the right hand of God,
and having received from the Father the *promise of the Holy
Spirit*, He poured out this which you now see and hear."

Acts 2:33

Today, God still gives the Holy Spirit to those who ask for His
indwelling. Jesus said:

"And I will pray the Father, and He will give you another
Helper, that He may abide with you forever, even the
Spirit of truth...."

John 14:16-17

What Is the Purpose of this Baptism?

The Baptism in the Holy Spirit is an anointing or endowment of
power from God. This anointing enables you, as a believer, to be a
more effective witness of the life of Jesus Christ. In this baptism, God
pours out His Holy Spirit to empower you so you can demonstrate
the life and ministry of Jesus, today. Jesus explained:

"But you shall receive power when the Holy Spirit has come upon you; and you shall be witnesses to Me in Jerusalem, and in all Judea and Samaria, and to the end of the earth."

Acts 1:8

God supernaturally gives the Holy Spirit to believers to equip and empower us to worship Him. When He came upon the early Christians, the first action of the Holy Spirit was to speak the praises of God through them.

"Cretans and Arabs—we hear them speaking in our own tongues the wonderful works of God."

Acts 2:11

Speaking in tongues is a way believers may praise and magnify the Lord as often as we wish. It is the release of our hearts overflowing in prayer and praise to God.

The Gentiles in the house of Cornelius magnified the Lord when the Holy Spirit came upon them.

...They heard them speak with tongues and magnify God....

Acts 10:46a

How Do You Receive this Baptism?

There are two requirements to receive the Baptism in the Holy Spirit.

1. You must be a child of God.

The Bible says that the world (unbelievers) cannot receive the Holy Spirit. Speaking of the Holy Spirit, our Comforter or Helper, Jesus said:

"Even the Spirit of truth, whom *the world cannot receive,* because it neither sees Him nor knows Him; but you know

Him, for He dwells with you and will be in you."

John 14:17

2. You must ask the Father in Jesus' Name to baptize you in the Holy Spirit.

Ask and you will receive. This baptism is for every believer. Anyone who asks for the Baptism in the Holy Spirit will receive this heavenly gift. The Word of God promises that you will not receive a counterfeit gift, but the real Holy Spirit. Jesus assured His followers:

> "For everyone who asks receives, and he who seeks finds, and to him who knocks it will be opened.
>
> "If a son asks for bread from any father among you, will he give him a stone? Or if he asks for a fish, will he give him a serpent instead of a fish?
>
> "Or if he asks for an egg, will he offer him a scorpion?
>
> "If you then, being evil, know how to give good gifts to your children, how much more will your heavenly Father give the Holy Spirit to those who ask Him!"

Luke 11:10-13

You do not have to persuade God to keep His Word. He longs for His people to receive this gift. Remember, Jesus said that our Heavenly Father would give the Holy Spirit to those who ask Him. You can have confidence that God will fill you with the Holy Spirit, because His Word says He will.

> Now this is the confidence that we have in Him, that if we ask anything according to His will, He hears us.
>
> And if we know that He hears us, whatever we ask, we know that we have the petitions that we have asked of Him.

1 John 5:14-15

This Baptism Is His Will for All Believers

When you ask the Father for the Baptism in the Holy Spirit, He will do it. His will is that you overflow continually with His Spirit. The Word says that believers are to understand (comprehend, grasp, and perceive) the will of God and be filled with the Spirit:

> Therefore do not be unwise, but understand what the will of the Lord is.
> And do not be drunk with wine, in which is dissipation; but be filled with the Spirit.
>
> Ephesians 5:17-18

What Happens when You Receive this Baptism?

1. You receive rivers of living water.

When you receive the Holy Spirit, He enters your innermost being (spirit) and begins to flow out like a river. Jesus explained this when He also said that His believers should receive the Holy Spirit:

> …"If anyone thirsts, let him come to Me and drink.
> "He who believes in Me, as the Scripture has said, out of his heart will flow rivers of living water."
> But this He spoke concerning the Spirit, whom those believing in Him would receive; for the Holy Spirit was not yet given, because Jesus was not yet glorified.
>
> John 7:37-39

2. You speak with other tongues—a new prayer language.

There is biblical evidence when the Holy Spirit fills you. In this baptism, God gives a supernatural language to you. This turns your heart more completely to Him. The initial biblical evidence of the baptism in the Holy Spirit is speaking with other tongues in a prayer language to God.

And they were all filled with the Holy Spirit and began to speak with other tongues, as the Spirit gave them utterance.

Acts 2:4

The people of Ephesus also spoke in tongues when the Holy Spirit came upon them:

And when Paul had laid hands on them, the Holy Spirit came upon them, and they spoke with tongues and prophesied.

Acts 19:6

Who spoke with tongues here? Does the Bible say that the Holy Spirit spoke with tongues? No. You will not read anywhere in the Bible that the Holy Spirit spoke with tongues. **The Bible says that the *people* pray in the Spirit and speak with tongues.**

What is the result then? I will pray with the spirit, and I will also pray with the understanding. I will sing with the spirit, and I will also sing with the understanding.

1 Corinthians 14:15

How can you release the power of praying in a new prayer language? **The believer speaks in other tongues in his prayer language to God by an act of his own will.** God does not make you speak in new tongues. He never forces anyone to speak in tongues, but He gives this gift to all who ask. God wants to bless His children.

For it is God who works in you both to will and to do for His good pleasure.

Philippians 2:13

Jesus said that speaking in other tongues is one of the signs that would follow those who believe:

"And these signs will follow those who believe...they will speak with new tongues."

Mark 16:17

When you pray in tongues, you will speak words that you do not understand. Although you are fluent in one or more languages, you will pray in a language you have never heard before. Your mind will not understand the words. Realize that your spirit is praying to God in the Holy Spirit's language:

For he who speaks in a tongue does not speak to men but to God, for no one understands him; however, in the spirit he speaks mysteries.

He who speaks in a tongue edifies himself.

1 Corinthians 14:2, 4a

Tongues are for your spiritual edification.

When you speak in tongues, the Holy Spirit reminds you of His indwelling presence. As we studied earlier, Jesus said:

"Even the Spirit of truth...you know Him, for He dwells with you and will be in you."

John 14:17

When you speak in tongues, you are praying according to God's perfect will:

Likewise the Spirit also helps in our weaknesses. For we do not know what we should pray for as we ought, but the Spirit Himself makes intercession for us with groanings which cannot be uttered.

Now He who searches the hearts knows what the mind

of the Spirit is, because *He makes intercession for the saints according to the will of God.*

Romans 8:26-27

You stimulate your faith when you pray in tongues:

> But you, beloved, building yourselves up on your most holy faith, praying in the Holy Spirit.

Jude 1:20

Praying in tongues brings spiritual refreshing to you:

> For with stammering lips and another tongue
> He will speak to this people,
> To whom He said, "This is the rest with which
> You may cause the weary to rest,"
> And, "This is the refreshing"....

Isaiah 28:11-12

Speaking in tongues tames your tongue and enables you to stay free from worldly contamination as you speak God's divine secrets.

> But no man can tame the tongue. It is an unruly evil, full of deadly poison.

James 3:8

You can build yourself up—become strong—by quietly speaking to God in other tongues wherever you are. For example, you can do this in a car, bus, or airplane. Or you can pray in tongues at home and on the job. You will disturb no one, if you do this privately.

Speaking in tongues keeps you so strong and in such close fellowship with Christ that you will not desire the world's temptations. It helps prevent you from submitting to the values of unbelievers around you. As we have discussed, you shall receive power after the Holy Spirit has come upon you. You will walk in a dimension of God's supernatural power.

Ask for the Baptism in the Holy Spirit

Right now, if you have not already done so, pray this simple prayer to receive the baptism in the Holy Spirit:

> **Father, I am Your child. Jesus is Lord of my life. Now, I ask You to fill me with the Holy Spirit. I receive the Spirit of God. By faith, now, I am Spirit-filled. Thank You!**
>
> **As a decision of my will, I now choose to speak to You, Father, with new tongues. My mind will not understand, but in obedience I release this prayer language. Holy Spirit, pour out through me as I speak in new tongues. In Jesus' Name. Amen!**

Now, begin to pray aloud to God in new tongues. Always remember the Holy Spirit releases God's power!

Expect the "Gifts of the Spirit"

The release of God's presence manifests in nine distinct major areas called the "gifts of the Holy Spirit." Now that you have received the Baptism in the Holy Spirit, these gifts will begin to operate in and through your life. Expect it daily. The nine gifts of the Holy Spirit are listed in the following passage of Scripture:

> But the manifestation of the Spirit is given to each one for the profit of all:
> for to one is given the *word of wisdom* through the Spirit, to another the *word of knowledge* through the same Spirit,
> to another *faith* by the same Spirit, to another *gifts of healings* by the same Spirit,

to another the *working of miracles*, to another *prophecy*, to another *discerning of spirits*, to another *different kinds of tongues*, to another the *interpretation of tongues*.

But one and the same Spirit works all these things, distributing to each one individually as He wills.

1 Corinthians 12:7-11

These nine gifts of the Spirit can be classified into three categories:

1. **Gifts of Revelation—gifts that "know" something.**
   Word of Wisdom: The supernatural revelation of part of God's plan and purpose for the future.
   Word of Knowledge: The supernatural revelation of facts concerning people, places, or things. It may be about the present or the past.
   Discerning of Spirits: A supernatural revelation into the spirit realm; seeing or discerning the Father God, Jesus Christ, the Holy Spirit, God's angels, Satan, demons, and the human spirits of men.

2. **Gifts of Power—gifts that "do" something.**
   Special Faith: A supernatural endowment (gift) from the Holy Spirit, promising that one eventually will receive what man asks or that which God speaks.
   Working of Miracles: A supernatural intervention in the ordinary course of nature; a temporary suspension of natural order; an interruption of nature, as we know it, by the power of the Holy Spirit.
   Gifts of Healings: The supernatural healing of a sick person. The Holy Spirit gives this without the means of any natural intervention.

3. **Gifts of Inspiration—gifts that "say" something.**
    Prophecy: A God-inspired supernatural utterance (a person speaking) in a *known* language, which edifies, comforts, or exhorts.
    Different Kinds of Tongues: A God-inspired supernatural utterance in an *unknown* tongue. This gift is *not* your private prayer language in tongues. Instead, it is spoken out in a public assembly for the interpretation to come forth for the benefit of gathered believers.
    Interpretation of Tongues: A God-inspired supernatural utterance in a *known* language, which explains the meaning of an *unknown* tongue previously spoken. Tongues and interpretation are equal to prophecy in their effect.

Spend time alone, right now. Pray in a new tongue before the throne of God. After a period, sit quietly. Ask God to speak the interpretation of what His Spirit is saying to you.

> Therefore let him who speaks in a tongue pray that he may interpret.
>
> 1 Corinthians 14:13

The interpretation could be the Spirit of God comforting your heart in a situation you are facing. Or it could be the Spirit empowering and calling you to perform an exploit of God for His glory. Whatever He does, you have stepped into a new dimension in God. Hallelujah!

Scriptural Confessions of Faith

Read the following Scripture again and confess it aloud (in bold letters). Always remember this Word from Jesus. This secret empowers you to walk victoriously in life:

> "But you shall receive *power* when the Holy Spirit has come upon you; and you shall be witnesses to Me in Jerusalem, and in all Judea and Samaria, and to the end of the earth."

Acts 1:8

Father, earlier, I asked You to fill me with Your Holy Spirit. I thank You, again, that You honored my request. Now, I walk in Your anointing and power to be a witness of Jesus in my city, state, nation, and the world. Use me, Father, as You desire, to move in the gifts of Your Holy Spirit. Let me be an instrument that demonstrates Your love and power to a hurting and lost world. Thank You for the privilege and honor of serving You. In Jesus' Name. Amen.

4

Freedom through Forgiveness and Reconciliation

Are some of your family members not speaking to each other? In your own workplace, have you found harbored attitudes and deep resentments against other employees or supervisors? Are unforgiveness, resentment, or bitterness robbing your life of the fulfillment that God desires for you? Do these feelings steal your peace and joy from your relationships with others?

The Holy Spirit has given an answer in the Word. The voice of God is calling the church today to forgiveness and reconciliation.

As you journey down The Victorious Walk, you will free and empower yourself to be a minister of forgiveness to others. You will learn principles of how to forgive others, release hurts, reconcile relationships, and restore what these hurts have stolen. You will see that restoration of the years lost through the pain and suffering of broken relationships is possible.

Free Yourself from Hindrances

Unforgiveness, resentment, and bitterness in your heart toward others will hinder your spiritual growth. If you do not forgive people who offend you, it will prevent you from experiencing the joy and fulfillment God wants you to have. You also will give Satan an opportunity to torment your mind.

In the Bible, *offend* means "the trigger of a trap." When you feel offended, you trap yourself into a hindering mindset. You continually rehearse how others have hurt you and scheme of ways to protect yourself from future harm. Satan is quick to oblige you by calling attention to the hurts others inflict. Again and again, he will bring thoughts of these offenses to you like a broken record.

Offended people put up walls to prevent their future vulnerability. Is this you? God wants to break down the wall, heal the hurt, and restore you to a place of transparency, vulnerability, and touchableness in Him.

Always Forgive Others

When Peter asked Jesus how often he should forgive, Jesus had an unexpected answer:

> Then Peter came to Him and said, "Lord, how often shall my brother sin against me, and I forgive him? Up to seven times?"
>
> Jesus said to him, "I do not say to you, up to seven times, *but up to seventy times seven.*"
>
> Matthew 18:21-22

This means at least 490 times for one offender! Without the Word of God as your foundation, this is impossible.

The Bible lays out a step-by-step process, teaching us how to forgive. It is very important that you understand these steps. Many people falter, because they do not follow all the steps of forgiving. For instance, sometimes they forgive in their own strength instead of invoking the presence of Jesus to forgive through His Name and Person.

Listed below are the biblical steps to forgive others, and regain and maintain proper relationships with them.

1. Recognize that by the blood of Jesus Christ, God forgives all your sins.

"But this is the covenant that I will make with the house of Israel after those days, says the LORD: I will put My law in their minds, and write it on their hearts; and I will be their God, and they shall be My people.

"No more shall every man teach his neighbor, and every man his brother, saying, 'Know the LORD,' for they all shall know Me, from the least of them to the greatest of them, says the LORD. For I will forgive their iniquity, and their sin I will remember no more."

Jeremiah 31:33-34

But this Man [Jesus], after He had offered one sacrifice for sins forever, sat down at the right hand of God.

Hebrews 10:12

2. Believe that the same Blood of Jesus, which forgives you, also forgives those who offend you.
If God forgives them, then only Satan can be their accuser.

And be kind to one another, tenderhearted, forgiving one another, just as God in Christ also forgave you.

Ephesians 4:32

3. By an act of your will, in the Name of Jesus, sincerely choose to forgive those who have hurt or offended you.
Jesus, in ending His parable about forgiveness, said:

"Then his master, after he had called him, said to him, 'You wicked servant! I forgave you all that debt because you begged me.

'Should you not also have had compassion on your fellow servant, just as I had pity on you?'

"And his master was angry, and delivered him to the torturers until he should pay all that was due to him.

"So My heavenly Father also will do to you if each of you, from his heart, does not forgive his brother his trespasses."

Matthew 18:32-35

And whatever you do in word or deed, do all in the name of the Lord Jesus, giving thanks to God the Father through Him.

Colossians 3:17

4. Recognize that you are forgiving through the Person of Jesus Christ, who lives in you.

If you do not do this, Satan can torment you by revisiting an old hurt over and over. Paul said:

Now whom you forgive anything, I also forgive. For if indeed I have forgiven anything, I have forgiven that one for your sakes in the presence of Christ, lest Satan should take advantage of us; for we are not ignorant of his devices.

2 Corinthians 2:10-11

5. Restore the same fellowship you had with the person before he offended you.

Interact with him as if it had never happened. By a decision of your will, forget the wrong that person has committed.

…"Their sins and their lawless deeds I will remember no more."

Hebrews 10:17

But if we walk in the light as He is in the light, we have fellowship with one another, and the blood of Jesus Christ His Son cleanses us from all sin.

1 John 1:7

6. Do not share your hurt with others.

If you tell others about offenses against you, they then pick up borrowed hurt. Also, do not pick up the borrowed hurt of another. This burden is not yours to carry. Reach out to others to help them become free from sin. Be sure they do not carry the guilt and reproach of others. Jesus said:

"If you forgive the sins of any, they are forgiven them; if you retain the sins of any, they are retained."

John 20:23

7. Pray this prayer aloud:

I, __(your name)__ , choose to forgive __(person's name)__ , as You forgave me, Lord Jesus. I forgive __(person's name)__ in the Name of Jesus and in the Person of Jesus. I now remit all __(person's name)__ 's sins through the shed Blood of Jesus, forgetting them as though they never happened. I release all hurt, in the Name of Jesus. Amen.

Now, check your heart. Is there anyone else you need to release, forgive, and forbear before the throne of God? Then, His grace can reach them as it has reached you.

8. Do not rehearse these offenses anymore.

After you have forgiven according to these biblical principles, it is only the devil who will bring the forgiven offenses and offenders to your mind. Do not allow this. You can stop him! Command him:

Satan, in the Name of Jesus, I bind you and command you to stop bringing these accusations to my mind!

Then, quote the following Scriptures to him:

"And these signs will follow those who believe: In My name they will cast out demons; they will speak with new tongues."

Mark 16:17

Then I heard a loud voice saying in heaven, "Now salvation, and strength, and the kingdom of our God, and the power of His Christ have come, for the accuser of our brethren, who accused them before our God day and night, has been cast down."

Revelation 12:10

Therefore submit to God. Resist the devil and he will flee from you.

James 4:7

"Do not remember the former things, Nor consider the things of old."

Isaiah 43:18

As you follow these principles of forgiveness, all parties involved are free to mature in Christ Jesus. Then, you can flow in His plan and purpose for your life, and receive His blessings.

5
How to Receive Divine Healing

As we began this book, *The Victorious Walk*, you read the first part of the Scripture in which King David cried out:

> Bless the LORD, O my soul,
> And forget not all His benefits.
>
> Psalm 103:2

The next verse lists some of these "benefits":

> Who forgives all your iniquities,
> Who heals all your diseases.
>
> Psalm 103:3

Have you discovered God's benefit of healing your physical body? or, have Christians told you that healing is not for today? Have they explained that God's power has left us on the earth? Do they tell you to be subject only to doctors' knowledge and ability? Has your faith fleeted when you looked to the healing virtue of God?

This chapter will cause your faith to soar as you contact God for your healing. It also will help empower you to minister His healing to others. You will find that it is God's will for you to walk in health and vitality, free from sickness and disease!

What Is the Origin of Sickness?

> ...Through one man sin entered the world, and death through sin, and thus death spread to all men, because all sinned.
>
> Romans 5:12

43

Sin, sickness, disease, and death entered the world through Adam's disobedience. Before Adam and Eve sinned, they never knew sickness. However, after they sinned, all creation was subject to futility. They opened the door to mankind for Satan to enter. Adam's and Eve's fall affected everything in the universe.

As a believer, you must settle in your heart that Satan—not God—is the originator of sickness and disease. Jesus said:

> "The thief [Satan] does not come except to steal, and to kill, and to destroy. I have come that they may have life, and that they may have it more abundantly."
>
> John 10:10

The devil's plan is the oppression and destruction of man:

> "...God anointed Jesus of Nazareth with the Holy Spirit and with power, who went about doing good and healing all who *were oppressed by the devil,* for God was with Him."
>
> Acts 10:38

God had a supernatural alternative to the devil's plan for man!

God Is Your Healer

Sometimes when people are sick, they seek the Lord. He may meet them (answer their prayers) in special ways. Then, they think God made them sick to teach them lessons. Nothing could be further from the truth! Satan, not God, afflicts us with disease. Sin (following Satan's way) can open the door to sickness. **God does not cause sickness to come upon us.**

God's Names in the Bible express His character. One of God's Hebrew Names is *Jehovah Rapha,* which means **"God, the Healer."** He refers to Himself as "the Healer," because He does heal. God revealed this aspect of His character in Exodus when He declared:

> …"For I am the LORD who heals you."
>
> Exodus 15:26

Jesus Healed the Sick

Study the life of Jesus in the Bible. During His earthly ministry, He reflected the perfect will of the Father.

> "For I have come down from heaven, not to do My own will, but the will of Him who sent Me."
>
> John 6:38

Jesus said He did nothing of Himself, but sought the will of the Father:

> "I can of Myself do nothing. As I hear, I judge; and My judgment is righteous, because I do not seek My own will but the will of the Father who sent Me."
>
> John 5:30

> Then Jesus said to them, "When you lift up the Son of Man, then you will know that I am He, and that I do nothing of Myself; but as my Father taught Me, I speak these things."
>
> John 8:28

A major portion of Jesus' ministry dealt with healing the sick. Jesus healed every kind of disease and sickness.

> And Jesus went about all the cities and villages, teaching in their synagogues, preaching the gospel of the kingdom, *and healing every sickness and every disease among the people.*
>
> Matthew 9:35

Large crowds of people went to see and hear Jesus.

> Then great multitudes came to Him, having with them those who were lame, blind, mute, maimed, and many others; and they laid them down at Jesus' feet, *and He healed them.*

> Matthew 15:30

Jesus healed everyone who touched Him.

> And when the men of that place recognized Him, they sent out into all that surrounding region, brought to Him all who were sick, and begged Him that they might only touch the hem
> of His garment. *And as many as touched it were made perfectly well.*

> Matthew 14:35-36

Multitudes of people followed Him, and He healed all who were sick.

> But when Jesus knew it, He withdrew from there; and great multitudes followed Him, *and He healed them all.*

> Matthew 12:15

Jesus is the will of God in action. He healed while He was on earth. Jesus did the will of the Father who sent him.

It Is God's Will to Heal You

When you were saved, your body became the temple of the living God. Therefore, sickness has no right to dwell in your body.

God wants you well! Jesus cares about your spiritual *and* physical health. He wants your body as free from Satan's influence as your spirit is.

Beloved, I pray that you may prosper in all things and be in health, just as your soul prospers.

3 John 1:2

God bought you with the Blood of Jesus. Jesus paid the price for your spiritual and physical health.

For you were bought at a price; therefore glorify God in your body and in your spirit, which are God's.

1 Corinthians 6:20

God wants you healed. He wants you well. He wants you whole. You must accept these truths in your heart. If you expect to receive from the Lord, you cannot approach healing (or anything else) with a double-minded, wavering attitude.

But let him ask in faith, with no doubting, for he who doubts is like a wave of the sea driven and tossed by the wind.

James 1:6

Study God's Word until you know without a single doubt that it is His will to heal you.

Jesus Is Willing to Heal You

When He had come down from the mountain, great multitudes followed Him.

And behold, a leper came and worshiped Him, saying, "Lord, if You are willing, You can make me clean."

Then Jesus put out His hand and touched him, saying, "*I am willing;* be cleansed." And immediately his leprosy was cleansed.

Matthew 8:1-3

Jesus' will is to heal everyone. He does not give to one person, while ignoring another. Jesus is not partial. He will heal all who ask, believe, and receive in faith.

> Then Peter opened his mouth, and said: "In truth I perceive that God shows no partiality."
>
> Acts 10:34

As we studied, during Jesus' earthly ministry, compassion for the people stirred Him to tenderness. He healed the sick time after time, and extended God's hand of mercy to the afflicted.

It becomes clear that God yearns to meet every need of man. That includes you! A manifestation of the healing presence of Jesus occurs because **He loves you.**

Jesus Paid the Price for Your Healing

When Jesus died, He did more than take away your sins. He also took all your sickness and infirmity:

> *Surely he took up our infirmities [sicknesses]* and carried our sorrows [pains]…
>
> But he was pierced for our transgressions, he was crushed for our iniquities; the punishment that brought us peace was upon him, and *by his wounds we are healed.*
>
> Isaiah 53:4-5 (NIV)

> That it might be fulfilled which was spoken by Isaiah the prophet, saying:
> "He Himself took our infirmities
> And bore our sicknesses."
>
> Matthew 8:17

Here, we see that Jesus paid the price for your sins *and* sickness on the cross of Calvary. This is in the Word of God. Settle in your heart that when God forgave you, He also healed you. Jesus Christ is your Healer. Believe it!

> Who Himself bore our sins in His own body on the tree, that we, having died to sins, might live for righteousness—*by whose stripes you were healed.*
>
> 1 Peter 2:24

Here, the Word of God says you "were healed" by His stripes. Jesus' enemies whipped Him, crowned Him with thorns, drove nails into His feet and hands, and thrust Him through with a sword! He finished His work. Jesus already has provided for your healing. When you plant that Word in you and witness the reality of Jesus' finished work for you, your days of sickness can be over!

Seek the Lord

Do not seek God only in a time of need, whether that need is for healing or something else. Instead, it is wise to pray and seek the Lord at *all* times, since He answers those who diligently seek Him.

> But without faith it is impossible to please Him, for he who comes to God must believe that He is, and that He is a rewarder of those who diligently seek Him.
>
> Hebrews 11:6

You Can Reap a Harvest of Healing

To reap your harvest of healing, begin by planting the seed of the Word about healing in your heart. Sometimes God heals you when someone else prays. However, you must plant your own crop of healing seeds—the Word of God—if you consistently want to enjoy divine health. If you have spent time planting God's Word in your heart, it will be there when you need it.

Your word I have hidden in my heart,
That I might not sin against You.

Psalm 119:11

Be attentive to God's Word and what it says about healing.

My son, give attention to my words;
Incline your ear to my sayings.
Do not let them depart from your eyes;
Keep them in the midst of your heart;
For they are life to those who find them,
And health to all their flesh.

Proverbs 4:20-22

Hear and Be Healed

Not only must you know what the Word of God says about healing, but you also must act on it. Remember, your faith without works is dead (James 2:26).

You gain knowledge about a person or ministry by hearing. People heard and saw Jesus heal the sick. That inspired them to go see Jesus teach, preach, and heal. They also took their sick relatives and friends to Him. Those who **heard** Jesus say that God had anointed Him to heal the sick believed Him and received their healing.

Then the report went around concerning Him all the more; and great multitudes came together to hear, and to be healed by Him of their infirmities.

Luke 5:15

Jesus taught the people, and then ministered healing. They *heard the Word* and *then were healed*.

And He came down with them and stood on a level

place with a crowd of His disciples and a great multitude of people from all Judea and Jerusalem, and from the seacoast of Tyre and Sidon, who came to hear Him and be healed of their diseases.

Luke 6:17

Jesus Is Still the Same Today

Jesus healed people because of His compassion. He never changes:

> Jesus Christ is the same yesterday, today, and forever.
> Hebrews 13:8

Jesus still heals, today. Compassion motivates Him to act on *your* behalf. He loves you as much as He loved the people He met during His earthly ministry.

Scriptural Confessions of Faith

Now, thank God for the faith, through the power of His Word, to be healed and walk in divine health.

Father God, I thank You that You have given to me all things that pertain to life and godliness. I thank You, Father, that You have given Jesus Christ to me. The Spirit of the living God is in demonstration today, because You have poured out Your Spirit upon all flesh. I thank You, that I am that flesh. You have poured Your Spirit upon me.

Lord, there is power in and through Your Word. As I meditate on what the Word says about healing, it transforms me. I also will see what You have done for me through Jesus' death. By His stripes I was healed!

Because of this provision from Jesus, I will walk in divine healing and in health. Not only will I receive

healing for myself, but I will minister healing to others in Jesus' Name. Amen.

The following Scriptures and prayers will build your faith for healing. Read the Scriptures first. Then, activate God's Word by praying aloud His promises about His divine healing power.

> "For as the rain comes down, and the snow from
> heaven,
> And do not return there,
> But water the earth,
> And make it bring forth and bud,
> That it may give seed to the sower
> And bread to the eater,
> So shall My word be that goes forth from My mouth;
> It shall not return to Me void,
> But it shall accomplish what I please,
> And it shall prosper in the thing for which I sent it."
>
> Isaiah 55:10-11

> He sent His word and healed them,
> And delivered them from their destructions.
>
> Psalm 107:20

Father God, Your Word contains all the power necessary to perform what You said You would do. Your Word is healing me now. The Word contains Your healing power, and it is working in me now. Thank You for sending Your Word to heal me.

> Who Himself bore our sins in His own body on the tree, that we, having died to sins, might live for righteousness—by whose stripes you were healed.
>
> 1 Peter 2:24

Father, I confess Your Word concerning healing. I believe I was healed by the stripes Jesus bore for me.

For the word of God is living and powerful, and sharper than any two-edged sword, piercing even to the division of soul and spirit, and of joints and marrow, and is a discerner of the thoughts and intents of the heart.

Hebrews 4:12

I thank You, Father God, that Your Word abides in me. It brings perfect soundness of mind and wholeness in body and spirit to me. This comes from the deepest parts of my nature and even goes to the joints and marrow of my bones.

He was despised and rejected by men, a man of sorrows, and familiar with suffering. Like one from whom men hide their faces he was despised, and we esteemed him not.

Surely he took up our infirmities and carried our sorrows [pains], yet we considered him stricken by God, smitten by him, and afflicted.

But he was pierced for our transgressions, he was crushed for our iniquities; the punishment that brought us peace was upon him, and by his wounds [stripes] we are healed.

Isaiah 53:3-5 (NIV)

That it might be fulfilled which was spoken by Isaiah the prophet, saying:

"He Himself took our infirmities
And bore our sicknesses."

Matthew 8:17

Father God, Surely Jesus has borne my sickness and disease and carried my pains. I do not have to carry what

Jesus already carried for me. He took my sickness upon Himself and bore my pains. Father, thank You for my healing.

Satan, I do not receive sickness, because Jesus bore it for me. By His stripes I was healed. Healing is mine now, in Jesus' Name.

Christ has redeemed us from the curse of the law, having become a curse for us (for it is written, "Cursed is everyone who hangs on a tree").

Galatians 3:13

Christ has redeemed me from the curse of the law. Sickness and disease are part of the curse of the law. Therefore, Jesus redeemed me from sickness and disease. His Blood ransomed me. I am free of disease, and refuse these symptoms. In Jesus' Name.

My son, give attention to my words;
Incline your ear to my sayings.
Do not let them depart from your eyes;
Keep them in the midst of your heart;
For they are life to those who find them,
And health to all their flesh.

Proverbs 4:20-22

Father, I will not let Your Word depart from before my eyes, for it is life to me. I have found it. Thank You that it is health and healing to all my flesh. In Jesus' Name. Amen.

6
Discover God's Abundance for You

You would not take on a project without first financially evaluating whether you could pay for it. No one would build a house without first determining if he had sufficient funds to build it. Similarly, no one would purchase a car without the funding or financing available to drive the car off the dealer's lot. So also, God does not give purpose and vision to your life without the provision to fund, support, and cause that vision to become fruitful.

As you journey with me through this last chapter of *The Victorious Walk*, you will discover the keys to release God's abundance into your life. You will learn that it is God's desire for you to walk in financial prosperity. For more information about this topic, please see my book *Millionaire Mentality*.

It Pleases God to Prosper You
Remember, the Bible says:

> Beloved, I pray that you may prosper in all things and
> be in health, just as your soul *prospers*.
>
> 3 John 1:2

You are entitled to financial abundance as much as to forgiveness and health. These are every Christian's God-given rights through Jesus. Do not listen to the devil's lies when he says you cannot have financial blessings!

God wants to bless you. He is able and willing to prosper you in all realms of life. Two biblical Names for God demonstrate this: *El Shaddai* (which means "the God who is more than enough") and *Jehovah Jireh* (which means "His provision shall be seen"). Because being your provider is part of His nature, it pleases God when He can prosper you!

> Let them shout for joy and be glad,
> Who favor my righteous cause;
> And let them say continually,
> "Let the LORD be magnified,
> Who has pleasure in the prosperity of His servant."
>
> Psalm 35:27

Choose Blessings, Not Curses

The Bible explains that obedience to God's Word releases blessings:

> "And all these blessings shall come upon you and overtake you, because you obey the voice of the LORD your God."
>
> Deuteronomy 28:2

In verses 3 through 14, you can read the blessings that God wants you to have.

On the other hand, disobedience to God's Word releases curses into your life:

> "But it shall come to pass, if you do not obey the voice of the LORD your God, to observe carefully all His commandments and His statutes which I command you today, that all these curses will come upon you and overtake you."
>
> Deuteronomy 28:15

You can find the curses in this same chapter in verses 16 through 68.

The choice is yours: Blessings or curses.

> "I call heaven and earth as witnesses today against you, that I have set before you life and death, blessing and cursing; therefore choose life, that both you and your descendants may live."
>
> Deuteronomy 30:19

Jesus Broke the Curse of Poverty for You

You don't have to settle for curses. Obey God's Word, accept Jesus' finished work for you at Calvary, and you can have a blessed life. Remember, Jesus paid the price to remove all the enemy's curses from your life.

> Christ has redeemed us from the curse of the law, having become a curse for us...that the blessing of Abraham might come upon the Gentiles in Christ Jesus....
>
> Galatians 3:13-14

Like sickness and sin, poverty is a curse, which Jesus broke when He died and rose from the grave. Jesus removed the curse of poverty from you.

> For you know the grace of our Lord Jesus Christ, that though He was rich, yet for your sakes He became poor, that you through His poverty might become rich.
>
> 2 Corinthians 8:9

Thank God that Jesus broke the curse for you! Because of that, you can **refuse to be denied the blessing of God.** Tell the devil to take his hands off the blessings God has provided for you. **He has no right to hinder or stop you from receiving what God has given to you.** Declare what is yours.

You can rightfully declare the blessings of Abraham in your life.

> Abram was very rich in livestock, in silver, and in gold.
>
> ...And the LORD had blessed Abraham in all things.
>
> Genesis 13:2; 24:1

God Empowers You with Prosperity

The financial anointing to create wealth is yours, but the purpose of wealth must be to further His Gospel!

> "And you shall remember the LORD your God, for it is He who gives you power to get wealth, that He may establish His covenant which He swore to your fathers, as it is this day."
>
> Deuteronomy 8:18

God never planned for you to have a stagnant well. He desires for you to have a flowing river of financial supply! This means that finances need to flow not only *to* you, but also *through* you. Jesus commanded:

> "Give, and it will be given to you: good measure, pressed down, shaken together, and running over will be put into your bosom. For with the same measure that you use, it

will be measured back to you."

Luke 6:38

Take These Steps, Today

As you continue your journey on The Victorious Walk, take these steps:

1. Become involved in a local church.

Find the local church, which will build your family's faith to carry out the visions and purposes of God. Look for a body of believers with a big heart for local and world missions. The Bible says God gives you power to get wealth that He might establish His covenant. Make sure it is a soul-winning and a giving church.

2. Tithe regularly.

Take a tenth of your earnings every week—or as often as you receive income—and tithe it faithfully to your local church. As you tithe, prove God and believe He will open the windows of Heaven. Believe this passage from Malachi:

> "Bring all the tithes into the storehouse,
> That there may be food in My house,
> And prove Me now in this,"
> Says the LORD of hosts,
> "If I will not open for you the windows of heaven
> And pour out for you such blessing
> That there will not be room enough to receive it."

Malachi 3:10

Until you find a local church, sow your seeds into this ministry: Jesus Experience at P.O. Box 10050 in Wilmington, DE 19850 U.S.A. This global ministry is good, hot soil to sow your tithe into. Then, when you find a local church that feeds you, pay your tithe there.

3. Give liberally above your tithe to world missions.

I encourage you to sow into Jesus Experience for your missions offering. We minister the Gospel globally, teaching, preaching, and healing in Bible campaigns. Annually, hundreds of Bible Colleges are open and empowering thousands of students to minister God's Full Gospel.

Do not shortchange God and yourself by giving only tithes. The Word of God says:

> "Will a man rob God?
> Yet you have robbed Me!
> But you say,
> 'In what way have we robbed You?'
> In tithes *and offerings*.
> You are cursed with a curse,
> For you have robbed Me,
> Even this whole nation."
>
> Malachi 3:8-9

The Bible declares that curse comes when a person does not give tithes *and* offerings.

Be Obedient and Faithful

Be faithful to your local church—faithful in your attendance, prayer, tithes, and offerings. Be a committed partner, supporting world missions. Be obedient to the Word of God. Then you can remind God, and reassure yourself, that He will fulfill all His promises to you. As you build *His* house, He will build *your* house.

Scriptural Confessions of Faith

Boldly declare and pray the following Scriptures. Claim all the financial blessings promised in God's Word. Remember, you can boldly declare His Word and proclaim His blessings over *every* area of your life!

> Thus says the Lord, your Redeemer,
> The Holy One of Israel:
> "I am the LORD your God,
> Who teaches you to profit,
> Who leads you by the way you should go."
>
> Isaiah 48:17

Thank You, Father, for teaching me to profit, and leading me in the way that I should go.

> "Give, and it will be given to you: good measure, pressed down, shaken together, and running over will be put into your bosom. For with the same measure that you use, it will be measured back to you."
>
> Luke 6:38

God, as I increase the measure of my offering, with the same measure You give back to me: good measure, pressed down, shaken together, and running over. I have abundance, and I have no lack. I thank You, Father, that You surround me with Your favor. As I give, men give unto me. In Jesus' Name!

> "And you shall remember the LORD your God, for it is He who gives you power to get wealth, that He may

establish His covenant which He swore to Your fathers, as it is this day."

Deuteronomy 8:18

Father, Your Word declares that You give power to get wealth so Your covenant may be established here on earth. I thank You for giving me power to release the financial anointing, so I can be a blessing to Your Kingdom here on earth.

Beloved, I pray that you may prosper in all things and be in health, just as your soul prospers.

3 John 1:2

Let them shout for joy and be glad,
Who favor my righteous cause;
And let them say continually,
"Let the LORD be magnified,
Who has pleasure in the prosperity of His servant."

Psalm 35:27

Father, Your Word says that You want me to prosper and be in health, even as my soul prospers. I now declare that I am prospering in all areas of my life as I continue down The Victorious Walk! Thank You for blessing me. In Jesus' Name. Amen.

Appendix

Become a Student of God's Word with The School of Biblical Studies

Destroy Your #1 Enemy
Your #1 Enemy is on the prowl!
Your #1 Enemy knows more than you know!
Your #1 Enemy keeps you from complete fulfillment!
Your #1 Enemy has destroyed your past!
Your #1 Enemy breaks up families!
Your #1 Enemy is always with you!
Your #1 Enemy is…….shhhhhhhh! Don't tell anybody!
Your #1 Enemy is ignorance!
> What you **DON'T KNOW** will hurt you!
> Don't let it destroy your future like it has your past!

Remember that God's Word declares:

> My people are destroyed for lack of knowledge: because thou hast rejected knowledge, I will also reject thee….
>
> Hosea 4:6 (KJV)

Turn the page to find an exciting free offer, which will change your life!

Ignorance!!!!!!!!! You are destroyed NOW!!!!!!!!!

The School of Biblical Studies brings to life powerful truths that will unlock personal fulfillment in your God-given vision, family, finances, health, mental well-being, prayer, and much more.

By contacting Gary Whetstone Worldwide Ministries today, you will begin a journey into practical and simple answers. You won't believe how much you have missed all of these years. These impactive teachings bring to light the power of God's revelation knowledge and set you above all that is average and ordinary.

Study Options

Attend the School of Biblical Studies through the following programs:

EXTENSION SCHOOL in your own home through any of the following media formats:

1. Audio CDs (ACDs) for CD players and most DVD Players
2. DVDs for viewing on most DVD players
3. Video CDs (VCDs) for viewing on video CD and recent DVD players (for international use only)
4. MP3 audios

MAIN CAMPUS

You can attend school in a classroom setting offered at Victory Christian Fellowship

FREE ON-LINE

We offer the entire bible school **free** on-line as well. Whether you elect to take bible school at home, in a classroom setting or on the internet, all students receive the same curriculum.

Certificate and Diploma

A certificate and diploma will be awarded upon graduation from the junior and senior years of Biblical Studies. These units of study also may be transferred to a degree program.

JESUS EXPERIENCE
SCHOOL OF BIBLICAL STUDIES

This course will enlighten you as to your position of righteousness (right-standing) with God through Jesus Christ

FREE Online Course
Your Liberty in Christ

Once you receive and walk in His revelation you will be...

- · Able to stand in the presence of God
- · Without any sense of guilt
- · Without any sense of shame

- · Without any sense of fear
- · Without any sense of insecurity
- · Without any sense of inferiority

just as if sin never existed.

Righteousness revelation will change YOU - change the way you think and feel and revelatory knowledge will cause you to see it in a new way and experience the word of God in a very personal way.

Log onto our website at JesusExperience.com
Select "**FREE**" Your Liberty in Christ
Complete course registration information
you are now ready to start the course!
(302) 561-6817 or sbs@jesusexperience.com

BECOME A MENTOR

Become a Mentor and lead others into experiencing the Life of Jesus Christ.

Sign up TODAY at Mentor.JesusExperience.com

As a mentor you will receive notes, videos and training in bringing everyone you know into the experience of Jesus' Life living in and through them.

Life's Answers Teaching Series

The following is a partial listing of Dr. Gary V. Whetstone's teaching series on video and audio CDs for your study and spiritual growth. For a detailed catalog of materials from the *Life's Answers* teaching series, please visit our web site or contact us at:

Jesus Experience
P.O. Box 10050
Wilmington, DE 19850-0050 U.S.A.
Phone: (302) 561-6800 • Toll-Free: (800) 383-4223 • Fax: (302) 324-5448
Web Site: www.JesusExperience.com • Email: info@JesusExperience.com

Empowerment Series

These power-packed courses equip you for your successful Christian walk as you fulfill God's will and purpose for your life.

The Call of God with study guide	ACD /MP3
Effective Praise with study guide	ACD /MP3
Harvest Your Dreams with study guide	ACD /MP3
Harvesting God's Promises with study guide	ACD /MP3
How to Heal the Sick with study guide	ACD /MP3
It's Time to Seek the Lord with study guide	ACD /MP3
Know the Real You with study guide	ACD /MP3
Mobilizing Believers with study guide	ACD /MP3
Move with the Holy Spirit in Gifts and Power with study guide	
	ACD /MP3
The Power of God's	English study guide
Prophetic Purpose with study guide	MP3
	Spanish, no study guide
	MP3
The Prevailing Power of Prayer with study guide	ACD /MP3
Step Up and Reap with study guide	ACD /MP3
The Unshakable Foundation with study guide	ACD /MP3
What Is this Revival, Anyway? with study guide	ACD /MP3
What Is Your Gospel? with study guide	ACD /MP3
Which Path Do I Take? with study guide	ACD /MP3
Withstand the Storm	ACD /MP3

Freedom Series

Jesus' full liberation is unveiled! The revelation you will receive about using God's weapons for victorious living will set you free from every offense, attack, and distress the enemy tries to wage against you.

Assignment Against the Church: The Spirit of Offense with study guide	
	ACD /MP3
Blood-Bought Promises with study guide	ACD /MP3

Extracting the Gold from Life's Crises with study guide   ACD /MP3
Firestorm   ACD /MP3
Freedom from Insecurity & Inferiority—
Crowned to Reign as a King with study guide
  ACD /MP3
How to Harness Your Mind with study guide   ACD /MP3
How to Identify and Remove Curses with study guide
  ACD /MP3
The Journey from Frustration to Fulfillment with study guide
  ACD /MP3
Love's Transforming Power with study guide   ACD /MP3
Make Fear Bow with study guide   ACD /MP3
The Power of the Lord's Blessing with study guide   ACD /MP3
Victory in Spiritual Warfare   ACD /MP3

Family and Relationships Series

These series enable you to overcome conflicts, establish positive relationships, and bring God's visitation to your family.

How To Build the Communication Bridge with study guide
  ACD /MP3
Friendship! A Two-Way Harvest   ACD /MP3
God's Covenant with You and Your Family with study guide
  ACD /MP3
How to Fight for Your Family with study guide   ACD /MP3
Manpower: Challenge to the Man with study guide   ACD /MP3
Relationships: Your Ruin or Rejoicing with study guide   ACD /MP3
What God Has Joined Together with study guide   ACD /MP3

Finance Series

Through these courses, learn how to reap your harvest and be set free forever from financial lack.

Champion, Success Is Within Your Reach with study guide
  ACD /MP3
Freedom from Need-Domination through Purpose-Motivation with study guide
  ACD /MP3
God's Financial Harvest Plan with study guide   ACD /MP3
Millionaire Mentality with study guide   ACD /MP3
The Problem of Too Much with study guide   ACD /MP3
Purchasing & Negotiation with study guide   ACD /MP3
Reaping: Harvest Your Increase with study guide   ACD /MP3
Success in Business with study guide   ACD /MP3
Tap the Money Gap with study guide   ACD /MP3
True Success—How to Find the Field God Has Planted for You with study guide
  ACD /MP3

For a complete and current listing of all ministry resources please visit our website at JesusExperience.com or 1-800-383-4223.

Pastor Gary invites you to...

One of the fastest-growing churches on the U.S. East Coast!

Victory Christian Fellowship and Branch Church

Dr. Gary V. Whetstone

Dr. Gary V. Whetstone is the senior pastor and founder of Victory Christian Fellowship in New Castle, Delaware, and founder of Gary Whetstone Worldwide Ministries. Additionally, Pastor Gary has started a branch church in Dover, DE. He holds an earned doctorate in Religious Education.

Since personally experiencing God's miraculous deliverance and healing from drug addiction and mental illness in 1971, Dr. Whetstone has devoted his life to helping others experience freedom in every area of life through God's Word. Today, he frequently ministers around the world in churches, seminars, and evangelistic crusades. Gifted in teaching, Dr. Whetstone provides practical biblical instruction wherever he ministers and has seen God work powerful signs, wonders, and miracles. Hundreds of thousands have become born-again, Spirit-filled, healed, and set free.

Because of their great burden to minister to the local community, Pastor Gary Whetstone and his church have launched life-changing outreaches in several areas, including HIV/AIDS; substance and alcohol abuse; prison outreaches; food and clothing programs; and large evangelistic campaigns, such as the dramatic production "Jesus, Light of the World," which draws thousands of people annually.

Dr. Whetstone's passion is to see the Word of God cover the world as the seas cover the earth. This vision has been accomplished through many ministry outreaches. These include: sending mission and evangelism teams around the globe; radio and television broadcasting; ministry through the Internet; Prayer Command Centers; and the School of Biblical Studies. An extensive audio- and video-training program, this school equips Christians to experience God's presence and to understand the Bible. This training program has been established in hundreds of churches in North and South America, Australia, Europe, Asia, and Africa. In addition to local-church and international branch locations, the School of Biblical Studies is available to individuals on-line by extension in their homes through audio CDs, DVDs, MP3s, and for international use only VCDs. Currently, this biblical-study program is in English, but it will be available in Spanish and other languages in the future.

Dr. Gary Whetstone has appeared on many national and international radio and television programs and has authored key books. Among these are *The Victorious Walk, How to Identify and Remove Curses!, Make Fear Bow, Millionaire Mentality, Your Liberty in Christ, It Only Takes One,* and his personal testimony of miraculous deliverance and healing in *Conquering Your Unseen Enemies.* His numerous study guides are testaments to his gifting in practical biblical teaching and are available for use with his many video- and audio-teaching series. Several of these English materials are available (or will be in the future) in Spanish, French, and other languages.

God has gifted Dr. Whetstone with an incredible business sense, enabling him to publish a series of teachings including *Purchasing and Negotiations, Success in Business,* and *Millionaire Mentality,* which have aired on his radio and television programs, "Life's Answers." These broadcasts currently reach an audience of millions in the United States, in Europe, in Canada, and on the Internet.

Their two adult children and their spouses, Feb and Laurie Idahosa, Benin City, Nigeria, and Eric and Rebecca Whetstone, New Castle, DE all serve in full-time ministry with their children, Isaiah and Carmine Whetstone and Benson Victor Osarhumen Idahosa III affectionately called (Big Ben) who is in heaven with Jesus, and Faith Emmanuel Benson Idahosa IV – "Baby Feb," Nathaniel Benson Idahosa V, and their latest, Judah Victor Benson Idahosa VI are active in local and international outreaches for Jesus Christ.